for ____________________

LOVE

Published by Sellers Publishing, Inc.

161 John Roberts Road, South Portland, ME 04106

Visit us at www.sellerspublishing.com • E-mail: rsp@rsvp.com

ISBN-13: 978-1-4162-4568-1

Printed and bound in China.

10 9 8 7 6 5 4 3 2

LOVE

what is life without it?

poems by Rumi

SELLERS
PUBLISHING

The minute I heard my first love story,
I started looking for you,
not knowing how blind that was.
Lovers don't finally meet somewhere.
They're in each other all along.

you are within . . .

Arouse

Your breath touched my soul
and I saw beyond all limits.

I once had a thousand desires.
But in my one desire to know
you all else melted away.

We are one

the force of you

I was dead, then alive.
Weeping, then laughing.
The power of love came into me,
and I became fierce like a lion,
then tender like the evening star.

Love calls –
everywhere and always.
We're sky bound.
Are you coming?

let go and fly ...

Awake to love

What you seek
is seeking you.

Embrace you . . .

I want to see you.
Know your voice.
Recognize you when you first
come around the corner.

I want to sense your scent when I come
into a room you've just left.
Know the lift of your heel,
the glide of your foot.

Absorb you . . .

Kiss you

I want to become familiar with the way
you purse your lips
then let them part,
just the slightest bit,
when I lean in to your space
and kiss you.

I want to know the joy
of how you whisper "more."

In your light I learn how to love.
In your beauty, how to make poems.
You dance inside my chest
where no one sees you, but sometimes I do,
and that sight becomes this art.

Inspiration

Speak, and I will listen

The heart has its own language.
The heart knows
a hundred thousand ways
to speak.

I am your lover, come to my side,
I will open the gate to your love.
Come settle with me,
let us be neighbors to the stars.
You have been hiding so long,
endlessly drifting in the sea of my love.

I've found you

drunk on love

Love is a river.
Drink from it.

To live without you
is to be robbed of love
and what is life without it?
To live without you
is death to me, my love
but some call it life.

You are inside of me

protect

I will soothe you and heal you,
I will bring you roses.
I too have been covered with thorns.

This is how I would die
into the love I have for you:
As pieces of cloud dissolve in sunlight.

At the end of my life, with just one
breath left, if you come,
I'll sit up and sing.

glory in all

This is love:
to fly toward a secret sky,
to cause a hundred veils to fall each moment.
First to let go of life.
Finally, to take a step without feet
and to disregard what appears to be the self.

Heart, I said, what a gift it has been
to enter this circle of lovers,
to see beyond seeing itself,
to reach and feel within the breast.

now i know

Awe

Your magnificence
has made me a wonder.
Your charm
has taught me the way of love.

You've seen my descent,
now watch my rising.

eternal ebb and flow

Refuge

Lovers find secret places
inside this violent world
where they may interact
with beauty.

Let yourself be silently drawn
by the strange pull
of what you really love.
It will never lead you astray.

Listen

love is not furtive

Love is an open secret,
the most obvious thing in the world
and the most hidden, with no why
to how it keeps its mystery.

Love is not an emotion,
it's your very existence.

honor it

No end to love

Come, sweetheart,
let's adore one another
before there is no more
of you and me.

I came back to You
because I could not find
the kind and decent things I found
in You anywhere else.

return to love

reveal yourself

Open to me, so that I may open.
Provide me your inspiration
So that I might see mine.

The real beloved
is your beginning and your end.
When you find that one,
you'll no longer expect anything else.

I am full

Learn

Love is the religion, and the universe is the book.

I am so small I can barely be seen.
How can this great love be inside me?
Look at your eyes, they are small
but they see enormous things.

The wonder of it

I am with you always

The sky was lit by the splendor of the moon,
so powerful I fell to the ground.
Your love has made me sure
I am ready to forsake this worldly life
and surrender to the magnificence of your being.